Woman by Design
Woman on Purpose

A CATALYST TO VALUE YOUR VOICE
& WALK IN YOUR WORTH!

Dr. Renee Allison

Unless otherwise noted, all Scripture references are from the HOLY BIBLE, KING JAMES VERSION, 1972, 1976, 1979, 1983, 1984, 1985 Thomas Nelson Inc., Publishers.

Woman By Design
Woman on Purpose
A Catalyst to Value your Voice and Walk in your Worth!

Dr. Renee Allison
New Life House of God World Outreach Ministries
P.O. Box 626 • Hammond, Indiana 46324
219-554-9455 • womanbydesign83@yahoo.com

Copyright 2009
Life Productions
A division of New Life House of God World Outreach Ministries

ISBN #978-1-943343-26-3

Designed and Published by:
Heavenly Enterprises Midwest, Ltd.
Chicago, Illinois • 773-783-2981
service@heavenlyenterprises.com

Dedication

I owe my life to my Heavenly Father. I agree with King David in Psalms 124, when he said, had it not been for the Lord, who was on my side, truly, I don't know where I would be. I Love the Lord with All my Heart!!

Second to God, is my amazing awesome, Husband, friend, power pusher, prayer partner and wonderful man of God, Apostle/Dr. Grant Allison III. He has been my constant friend for over 45 years and I thank him for the many years of sharing the awesome wisdom and revelation that the Lord gives him with me and the world. He is the sparkle in my eye, the skip in the beat of my heart, and the dimples in my smile. You are the catalyst that God has used to continue to open doors for me both naturally and spiritually. Thank you for all you do for me, our family, church family and the world.

Woman By Design ~ Woman On Purpose

I love YOU!

To our four children Deedra, Grant IV, Gregory, Geremie and spouses, I honor and love you all so much! You have brought so much Joy to my life through the years. I pray as I always have that you will Always please God and in doing that you will always please us! To Our ever increasing grandchildren 16 at the time of this writing and now 4 great grandchildren at the time of this writing, you are loved and appreciated!

To The church like no other, New Life House of God World Outreach Ministries church family, you are part of the stimulus for my life that pushes me and pulls on the anointing and grace that God has given me, and I thank you and I Love you so much!

Leaders in the body of Christ that have been a part and have given wisdom and support to me and my family includes; Apostle/Dr. I.V. and Pastor/Dr. Bridget Hilliard and the Hilliard family! You continue to lead by example, leaving lasting footprints and a light of faith for others to follow, Thank You! I Love You!

Last but certainly not least, my incredible, prophetic, prolific Mother Ruth, the most amazing mother any person could have, my wise Father Fred, great lover of God, my Brother Lavelle, whom I never met, Sisters,

Martha a rock and Ann all heart, who are all home in heaven. I love you! I thank you and I miss YOU! Your lives have lasting ripples that continue to make impact in our family and the world and to my remaining brothers, Fred, Sylvester, Lonnie, Henry, Leo and Jerome and my sister, Michele, I love you all!

Woman By Design ~ Woman On Purpose

Table of Contents

Foreword ix

Introduction xiii

Excavation 3

Woman by Design 17

Designer Original 29

Fashioned for Greatness! 41

Can't Take My Eyes off You!!! 53

All Dressed Up!!!! 65

Next Steps 75

My Prayer for You! 79

Woman By Design ~ Woman On Purpose

Foreword

A Woman by Design, Woman on Purpose is a woman that is going to rise UP and take her place using the Kingdom Authority that was given to her from GOD!!! Her desire is not to compete with the male man, but to demonstrate and walk in her own unique completeness, authority and assigned purpose in the earth given to her by GOD!

God has ordained and provided an inheritance for women especially those that are sanctified (set aside for His use). Sanctification is not just want she wears in the natural, but it is also speaking about what she wears in the spirit, her anointing! A Woman Designed on Purpose has learned to Value her Voice and Walk in her Worth given by God!

I have seen so many women, married; widowed; separated; single and divorced that are not being fulfilled. They have a hunger and yearnings in their heart, a mandate that God has placed on their life. They have, a gift, a call and yet, they have many times felt overlooked and confined by the restraints and constraints of man's opinion, religious philosophy and traditions. Some people have thought of women only as handmaidens, housewives, mothers, bus drivers, cooks, choir singers or many of the incredible roles women often function in. Although, women can operate in these areas of life they are purposed by God to also Rule, Reign and Govern. They should not have to operate with a flashlight leading from behind closed doors so others won't see who is really making decisions and walking in divine authority. God has called women on purpose to let their light shine so that men can see their good, no, great works and glorify God (Matthew 5:16)!

Let me just say my sister all the anointing that has been placed on the inside of you, is not just to lay hands on dishes, but the anointing comes to destroy yokes and set the captives free! God has made it clear in His Word, He blessed them! Although some of the roles men and women function in are very different, His mandate to preach the gospel, to work in the ministry, to be instant in season and out has no gender tag on it (Gal 3:28); it has a submission to God tag!

In the following pages, my prayer is that women will come from the background and shadows of their lives and that men will remain secure in who he is and understand, encourage and esteem the women as they are both willing to submit to

God and each other in the fear of God (Ephesians 5:21). The Word of God says that we should submit ourselves one to another and in the book of Ephesians 4:13 it says, "…until we all come into the unity of the faith…" That includes **Women by Design, Women on Purpose!**

Prayer moment; Father we thank you for your precious women and we believe as your word says out of your belly shall flow rivers of living water! Father, We thank you for the flow of life and we receive it now in Jesus name!

Woman By Design ~ Woman On Purpose

Introduction

Dear Woman of God or Woman at large, I want to thank you for making a choice to read this book. In this day many would rather look the other way and act as if no gender challenges are facing us but not you, you decided to on purpose search for and recover your hidden pearls and wear them proudly as a woman. You know pearls are very special rare gemstones that are made from an irritant that found It's way inside of the oyster or shell they came out of! And so are you! The duration of development time depends on the type of pearl it is.

Freshwater pearls takes between 1 to 6 years and Salt water pearls from 5 to 20 years to develop. According to your faith it will be unto you, whatever the call of God is on your life and your willingness to acknowledge and yield to Him can determine the amount of time needed for your anointing to develop and manifest.

Like the pearls things come to irritate us but those very things can also development us into very precious gems. God gives us everything that we need that pertains to life and godliness (2 Peter 1:3), every single thing, we just have to believe it, receive it, obey His work, trust God and know the process is necessary to make us ready for the purpose or promise. We also have to know and understand if the process is from God or manmade.

Valuing and honoring the heart of women has been such a very special area of ministry to me for many years. The more I study us, the more I thank God that he made us on purpose and I want to know more about us. God's word says that we are fearfully and wonderfully made (Psalm 139:14) men too, that means that God thought enough of us to divinely design form and fashion us on purpose, so that we can make an impact in the earth. He made us distinct by design and purpose.

As we walk faithfully according to His purpose for our lives, it will bring fulfillment to us individually, but it also brings such Glory and Honor to God as his presence fills the earth and ministers to others through us. I pray that you will allow this book to be a catalyst and the Holy Spirit to minister to your heart as His revelation knowledge unfolds truth to you today and release you into the fullness of God's original Purpose for you!

I Am Necessary!

Woman By Design ~ Woman On Purpose

Excavation

"My grace is sufficient for thee"

For centuries women have been told lies regarding the will of God for their lives for instance I once say a statement that, "Women in their greatest perfection were made to serve and obey man". Can you believe that?! That is an actual quote! In this chapter we are going to dig deep and confront and dispel some of those lies with scripture and provide for us the sword of the spirit which is the word of God (Ephesians 6:17).

Many women have felt, myself included, that their role in the work of the Lord is only because God couldn't find a willing man to get the job done so He had to settle for the next best thing, a substitute, a mere woman. You know when many think about a substitute, it's often categorized as second best, second class, less than, one that only fills in for the real deal, no voice of their own just a repeat of the person who's place they are taking.

There have been well known women of God that have been used mightily in the earth that have apologized for being a mere women including well known evangelist Kathryn Kuhlman.

Kathryn was one of the greatest evangelist in the world she loved and was used by God in a mighty way but of course being a woman, she had many unnecessary battles to fight some just because of her gender, she too was a Woman by Design, Woman on Purpose. Her spiritual legacy in part is that, she has provided footprints for walking with God by spending time with and through the leading of the Holy Spirit. Her great Love for God and her love for souls being saved and seeing people healed will march on through the halls of time. Pastor Benny Hinn, according to Hinn, is one of her proteges, often testifies how her life impacted his life and ministry today. Did she really know her value and worth as a woman of God?

Some women feel and have felt that they were an afterthought in God's plans. I believe that God saved the best for last. I believe God wanted to tell woman who they were before He brought her to the man (Adam) to see what he would name (call) her. The very definition of the word substitute suggests that it's a person or thing that acts or serves in place of another. God didn't put woman in place of the man we were in him from the beginning (Genesis 2:21). But wait, God uses substitutes! God, never in all of his splendor and glory makes mistakes. Sometimes people can be called something to dishonor them but when we look a little closer it might be the very thing that confers honor on them, therefore, let's revisit what a substitute might be in Gods eyes or from His perspective.

In the book of Genesis 22:13, Abraham was willing to sacrifice his promised seed Isaac. The very seed he got in trouble with God about because he didn't wait for God to manifest the promise between he and his wife Sarah or (Sara) at that time, decided to help God out and send Abram at the time into her handmaiden. Abraham tried to rush the process due to a lack of faith and patience. That was not the will of God? Gods' grace! After Abraham got new instructions, clearer instructions from God, waited on the promise seed his son Isaac from his wife Sarah and then God ask for him! God asked Abraham to sacrifice his son Isaac and of course even though he waited 25 years for him to be born, Abraham was willing. He had learned to trust God by this time and he was willing to obey God no matter what the price!

As Abraham raised his hand to sacrifice his son, (his promised seed), the scriptures says he raised his eyes and looked, and beheld the substitute!!! A Ram caught in the thicket (Genesis 22:13) to be the substitute, Wow! I am sure Abraham was so glad that God provided for him a substitute! Could you imagine the relief and joy that must have filled his soul as he saw the ram in the bush. Then of course we see Jesus, made a little lower than the angles (Hebrews 2:9) came down from being with the Father not because He was guilty of any crime or misdeeds, but because both God and Jesus knew, He would need to be used as a substitute.

When Jesus died on the cross He would be taking the punishment that we so easily deserved. No He did not deserve to die but He was willing to become our substitution! He that knew No sin would become sin for he that engaged in sin (2 Corinthians 5:21), what a substitute! I Peter 3:18 says, "the righteous for the unrighteous". There is a doctrine or teaching of substitutionary atonement which suggest that Christ suffered vicariously, Him being the substitute for the sinner, His life for ours. It also suggest that Christs sufferings were expiatory meaning, His sufferings made amends or to compensate for a wrongdoing. So if being a Woman on Purpose, means to be a substitute it's in line with the work of our elder brother Jesus the Christ, the Son of the Living God.

Let's go back to the beginning to get a clearer view of God's decree to mankind. Remember Adam walked with God when he named all the animals; she was right there in him. Genesis 5:1-2 says, "This is the book of the generation of Adam. In the day that God created man, in the likeness of God made he him; Male and Female created He them; and God blessed them and called their name Adam, in the day when they were created." When God saw it was not good for the man to be alone or (all-one) God took her out of him, and woman became the only living thing that was made from something that was already living, the account of creation clearly indicates this.

Genesis 2:18-24 tells us that God created the woman by removing a rib and fashioning it into a woman, some suggest that this was not part of the pair of 12 ribs that humans have but the original Hebrew word could mean or suggest that it was actually part of his side. I'm not clear on which method or body part God used but I do know ladies that we are here! Part of our redemption came as a result of Jesus being pierced in His side for us; I believe as usual that the final act just as we were formed last had something to do with being fully restored by the blood and water that came from His side!

Adam identified the woman that God made for him as an equal part of himself yet having different parts and functions; an added function of child bearing and nursing. Remember this was part of Gods original mandate and plan for them to be fruitful and multiply! Adam identified her ability to carry life, meaning she could bear or have children, but still he called her Woman, bone of my bone, the connective tissue that forms the major portion of the skeleton and flesh of my flesh, which is the surface or skin over the body. The same Adam that named all the animals, called Woman by her Purpose, Intention and Destiny! She was called woman because she has a womb not because she was inferior to him but she actually completed him. She was the answer to his loneness or all oneness; she was his fulfillment, suitable and adaptable for him because. She was framed, fashioned and purposed by God to be compatible just for him as a Woman by Design!

An untruth suggests, women were made to serve men as inferior partners. As we have stated previously, God formed and fashioned her because he (Adam) needed help, he was alone. The word of God says in I Peter 3:7, "Likewise, ye husbands dwell with them according to knowledge, giving honor unto the wife as unto the weaker vessel and being heirs together of the Grace of life; that your prayers be not hindered." God still holds Adam responsible for what he calls her, they are heirs together as ordained by God. God says giving honor unto the wife….so that your prayers won't be hindered. Of course we see the marriage relationship in this verse but remember the man was alone and God formed the woman to help him, in this verse this is just one of the ways that women can stand with their men in a relationship.

Again this scripture revealed that women were created by God as equal, joint-heirs of His grace. That's right ladies; we are equal heirs of God's grace. God's grace is the ability to do what God has called you to do. His grace has no gender affiliation but the amazing grace that God provides is actually the power and strength to become and do whatever you are purposed to do in the earth.

Several years ago after a service, I was prompted by the Holy Spirit to stay in the sanctuary when the service was over, as I began to walk around the sanctuary, I began to pray and the Holy Spirit said to me, "My Grace is Sufficient", I said, I know "He said not saving grace," I began to question what that meant because I had not heard of any other kind of grace at that point which was over 20 years ago. "He said my enabling ability to do what I've called you to do is sufficient for you." This word scared me and confused me because again, I had never heard of this kind of grace before.

I was so excited the Holy Spirit impressed me to read the scriptures where God was speaking to Apostle Paul in II Corinthians 12:9-10 which says, "My grace is sufficient for thee; for my strength is made perfect in weakness." Oh my god this scripture has given me insight in who I am as a woman and that I have not looked backed. I don't have to take a back seat because God's grace is enough, He will make all grace abound toward me and I will never come down from what God showed me. God has already provided for us everything that we need to walk as women; we don't have to be afraid we just need to obey.

There are many untruths as it relates to the rights of women such as; The untruth that says that women must find their ultimate purpose in a man. The truth is that women's ultimate purpose and fulfillment can only be discovered as they diligently seek to please God for we are complete in Christ

(Colossians 2:10). The word of God tells us in John 4, that Jesus had to go to a place called Samaria. While there he met a woman that came to the well to get water. This woman had been with several men actually married five of them and the current one that she was with was not her husband. Jesus new her situation that she was looking for love, fulfillment, happiness, joy, peace etc., He knew her plight.

Jesus said to the woman, "if you knew the gift of God, and who it is that is saying to you to Give me a drink; you would have asked him, and he would give you living water. My god, see it doesn't matter if you have a husband or have had many, Jesus will meet you where you are in your dry place to give you water to drink. He shows us that without Christ and walking in your purpose you have no living water. Our fulfillment as women comes as a result of knowing Him and knowing who we are in Him. Hebrews 11:6 says; "But without faith it is impossible to please Him; for he that cometh to God must believe that He is and that He is a rewarder of them that diligently seek Him," rewarder of them, not just him(male). Without air, we cannot breathe and without God truly we cannot live! This woman at the well found living water and her purpose, her voice, her value, her worth and her worship.

The father in spirit and He is seeking us to worship

him! The truth of her purpose was birth out right at the well in the middle of the day, water pot and all, she found the Christ and she found herself. She went into the town and told the men "come, see a man," that day revival broke out, a woman found value in her voice, began to walk in her worth because she was confronted with the truth of her condition, which set free and she in turned told everybody and the scriptures says, "and many of the Samaritans of that city believed on Him for the saying of the woman, which testified, He told me all that ever I did."

Another misdirection used by many to muzzle women suggests, that I Corinthian 14 which says, "Let your women keep silent in the church for it is not permitted unto them to speak; but they are commanded to be under obedience, as also saith the law.," This scripture, doesn't say all women should not speak or preach it dealth with the Corinthian church.

In Genesis 3:16 it says, "I will greatly multiply thy sorrow and thy conception; in sorrow thou shalt bring forth children and thy desire shall be to thy husband, and he shall rule over thee." I thank God for the blood of Jesus; we are not under the curse or the law but under GRACE. This scripture was a result of the curse and the fall. However, "Christ hath redeemed us from the curse of the law, being made a curse for us; for it is written, Cursed is every one that hangs on a tree: That the blessing of Abraham might come on the

Gentiles through Jesus Christ; that we might receive the promise of the Spirit through faith" (Galatians 3:13). God's original design for His creation is to bring and give Glory to Himself, not compete with each other for headship of each other but to be complete in Him!

A new day is here! It is a day of true revelation of God's Word: a day when a woman will assume her rightful position in the Body of Christ, and rise to the full height of her stature in spirit, soul and body. The truth of her purpose being revealed; that she is not to dominate man or be dominated by man, but to walk alongside him in the earth giving glory to God. Revelation is the uncovering of a truth that can and will bring understanding to the heart, mind and spirit of the hearer or reader. That's what God's Word is in this hour – a clear truth of His will that will set the captives free! We must be willing to allow the Holy Spirit to excavate the lies of the ages so the well of living water can flow freely from her. We shall know the truth, and that truth that we come to know and appropriate will set and keep us free! (John 8:32)

Confession:

Father I thank you that you have given me voice and value and made me free to walk in and be All that you purposed me to be. I Am Yours!

My Value is not Determined by the Things that I Possess, My Value is Determined by the One that Created, Designed and Sustains Me!

Woman By Design ~ Woman On Purpose

Woman by Design

God blessed them and said, "Be fruitful and multiply!"

One hot summer day at an outdoor Barbecue I was asked by one of the hosts of the event (happened to be the regional chairperson of an organization called Women of the Word International), what I thought about speaking at women's conference at that time I had spoken in many services but nothing that I would consider an actual conference. I was enjoying myself at the cookout and I had no reason to be guarded or concerned so I said well I am honored to do whatever God would want me to do, she then asked what I thought about speaking out of the country I responded I was willing to do whatever she needed me to do, little did I know that the woman had already given my name to a committee that was looking for a speaker for a women's conference.

Later that year In November/December 1999, I received an overseas call (initially I thought they had the wrong number) we hung up but the caller called right back and said they were referred to me by a woman they knew that was part of the Woman of the Word International and they mentioned the church that she was affiliated with in my area, that provided legitimacy and so I continued to listen to see what the call was regarding.

The Pastor said that they were having a Women's Conference and would I consider being the keynote speaker, Wow, I thought really going to the Dominican Republic to speak. My heart started racing and beating fast, but I still said that I would be open to it if it was the Lord's will. I told her that I would pray about our conversation and call her after I consider her invitation and would call her soon, she asked that I contact her as soon as possible so that they could make arrangements for me to arrive.

After consulting with my husband we agreed that I should go. I called the Pastor back and got additional information regarding the conference and then I asked the big question – what is your topic or theme? What did you want to accomplish? She said oh, I thought that you were going to give me a theme. I thought to myself, what kind of crazy is this? How can you have a conference and you don't even have a theme? She asked me what God was saying to my heart concerning women. Before she asked this question, I had not thought of what God wanted to say to or about women at all. I thought, I was not really thinking about women's ministry. I would minister to them all the time and God gave me specific words for women but before I could finish that thought and before I even knew it, the Holy Spirit spoke through my mouth and my response to her was...

"Woman by Design, Woman on Purpose! God began to say to her through me that women are not an afterthought, we are part of His original Design and His original Purpose! We are not an afterthought in the heart of God but we are a part of His original purpose.

She began to scream and get excited on the phone, that's it, that's it she said. My heart again began to race, I knew that the words coming out of my mouth were not my own but I believe, came from the heart of God. God was up to something then I felt something had just shifted inside of me. There was a change in my thinking a transformation was taking place regarding my purpose as a woman of God. I could not then and can not now get away from this assignment I thought about the theme all the time and it continues to grow today.

The process began for this word to snowball and when I hung up the phone, I said to myself, Oh my God, what did I say; what have I gotten myself into. The enemy began immediately speaking to my mind saying to me, people are going to call you Jezebel and your husband will be called Ahab because your trying to take the place of a man. Although the enemy was in my ear talking and breathing smoke, in my spirit I was so very sure I heard the voice of God and this was the Word of God. This was part of what I was engineered to do, this is part of my destiny, my Purpose to be a blessing to women worldwide proclaiming their inheritance and independence from bondage was being birthed in my spirit by the Holy Spirit.

Luke 4th chapter talks about how Jesus was led of the Spirit into the wilderness to be tempted by the enemy and then after he had gone through the time of testing He returned in the fullness of power of the Spirit and went to Nazareth. The bible says that Jesus went into the synagogue on the Sabbath and He stood up to read as they gave Him the book of the prophet Esaias or (Isaiah) as we would say.

Jesus read from the place in Isaiah that says, "The Spirit of the Lord is upon me, because He hath anointed me to preach the gospel to the poor; He hath sent me to heal the brokenhearted, to preach deliverance to the captives, and recovering of sight to the blind, to set at liberty them that are bruised,

To preach the acceptable year of the Lord." And then the bible says Jesus closed the book and the eyes of all of them were looking at Him (Luke 4:18). This is the scripture that God spoke to my heart many years before the invite to this conference and now I knew it would be fulfilled in my lifetime and the lives of many.

I started thinking of the possibilities of change for women to be set free, to be made whole and it was on! I was all in! God began speaking to my spirit regarding His plan for women not mine, I am in full agreement however, and He has never stopped! He said we are indeed "Women by Design, Women on Purpose!"

The plans on my end were being made, my husband agreed to accompany me on the trip, and as we share with other people they wanted to attend so I got an idea to invite others and I ended up taking a team of awesome ladies with us. We went to the conference in April 2000. The conference was scheduled to be a two day event starting on Friday April 21-22, 2000, however when I told the Pastor that invited me that we were coming in earlier they asked if my husband Dr. Grant and I would agree to do a couple radio spots/programs and also if we would like to speak in some of the local churches, which we agreed to do.

Originally we were going early because we had

never been to the Dominican Republic after doing a little research we were very interested about the country and the culture so we wanted to have some vacation time but that quickly went by the wayside after we told them when we were coming on Tuesday. After we arrived on Tuesday, we attended our first event on Tuesday evening speaking at some of the local churches and doing radio on Wednesday morning. By the time Friday came, the registration went from 150 expected registrations to they said to about 400-500. Now this was not supposed to be a very large event, but because of God's plan and His anointing, the Word of the Lord went out over the air waves and the conference grew.

The area that we were speaking in was a predominantly Spanish speaking area although the host of the conference were missionaries they were not Spanish therefore I had a local translator that was scheduled to translate for me during the conference. She was a beautiful lady and she accompanied me to all the radio stations and the churches in the evenings during the week so we had gotten to know each other pretty well she had become acquainted with how I flowed in ministry and I was expecting her to continue working with me during the conference when it started on Friday.

The conference was scheduled to be for women only, however, because my husband and I had ministered during the week at other churches, some of the men pastors wanted to attend. I was a little concerned about the male pastors wanting to attend because the enemy was of course saying they were not going to like what God wanted to do for the women at the service. I couldn't worry about it' I had to trust God that He gave me what He wanted me to say and He would be with me all the way through it. I got His Peace!

The conference host told the men that they were not allowed and they needed to leave. The first night was a buzz of excitement with people coming from everywhere. The grounds were on fire with excited people singing songs and the air was fueled with anticipation. The conference host got word that the drummer somehow couldn't make the meeting and they didn't know what the praise team was going to do without a drummer; they needed a drummer and low and behold my husband Dr. Grant said he would play the drums for them. That decision allowed not just him but a few other male pastors to stay for part of the conference, the host told them only the worship but of course they stayed for the entire event. The hall/conference center was filled to capacity; they had people coming in from the capital of Santo Domingo and several other surrounding cities so they could be a part of this event. The conference host was so excited that they decided to change the translator and get me one that normally works with well-known TV speakers they told me. I was not too happy about this because I liked and had gotten use to the person that was translating and speaking for me and I didn't really want any unnecessary changes. I was trying to stay focused on the word that God was going to bring through me.

When my team and I walked into the conference room, it was so very heavy with sadness and burdens. The women looked so overwhelmed with the cares of life. I couldn't explain the heaviness but it was overwhelming. The service started and praise and worship was very good my heart was beating fast. Remember I had a message that was not too popular in the United States and certainly I didn't know if it would be here either.

I didn't have a clue of how they would respond in another country to the word that God gave me concerning women. Although we preached during the week at other locations, I didn't share any of the messages about the call of God for women. When I was called up to minister the word of the Lord, Genesis 1:26-31 was the scripture text. In this text God tells us clearly that He made male and female in His image after His likeness to be like Him. The word of the Lord says, "And God said, Let us make man in our image after our likeness: and let them have dominion over the fish of the sea, and over the fowl of the air, and over the cattle, and over all the earth, and over every creeping thing that creepeth upon the earth. So God created man in his own image, in the image of God created he him; male and female created he them. And God blessed them, and God said unto them, Be fruitful, and multiply, and replenish the earth, and subdue it; and have dominion over the fish of the sea, and over the fowl of the air, and over every living thing that moveth upon the earth....And God saw everything that he had made, and behold, it was very good. And..." All He had made, that includes the woman and said He saw that it was very good!

Oh my God! You ae very good' you are made in the image and likeness of God and you are a "Woman by Design, a Woman on Purpose!" You are not an afterthought, you don't have to take a back seat but you must walk in the blessing of the Lord for your life on purpose. The women received the word from God as if they were being transfused. They responded to the Word of God as if life was being breathed into their lungs for the first time. The anointing of God was so very heavy, that evening that my new translator went out under the power of God within the first few minutes as I started to preach and was not able to finish the service; so guess what – I got my original translator back. Isn't God wonderful?! He knew who He wanted to assist me and who He wanted to use. Remember how Jesus sent His disciples out two by two. Of course I had nothing against the new translator she told me later when she apologized that she was just enjoying the presence and power of God so much that she could not stand up. Praise God!

Now remember when I got the call from the conference host in 1999, the enemy told me I was going to be laughed at. Well those women were not laughing; they were receiving and being changed by the power of God's word and purpose for their life. Needless to say, we had an alter call as a matter of fact my husband was concerned that I would be trampled because of the stampede of women that came to the altar and it was full of conversions and recommitments to Christ. God our originator, creator, faithful father, gave His women life and they still breathe today.

I like Moses, Jeremiah and many others in the word of God gave Him my limitation speech, I was scared! You know, I'm to this or that. I felt just like you might have at times; that I could not speak well, not because I didn't have the articulation of speech or the anointing of God on my life, but for me and many other women it was only because I was a woman!

I tried not to be too outspoken or overbearing up to that point. I was trying not to call attention to the call of God on my life. My husband would always encourage and push me to obey God no matter what, but at times I was still afraid of men. One day I even mentioned this to a man of God, Dr., I.V. Hilliard just in passing that I preached this message in 2000 and how I felt it was a hard message to minister. He, without hesitation said, "Don't you ever be afraid to say what God tells you to say." My heart was beating so fast, it shook me up a little because I knew God was speaking through him to speak to that fear of man that was trying to rise and correct me at the same time.

My husband Apostle Grant, has always encouraged me but I think sometimes when people really close to you give you words of wisdom we think they just don't want to hurt our feelings, now I know my husband will not sugar coat anything (he is straight up raw) as they say but this word was different coming from Dr. Hilliard, it shifted my thinking, my perspective and behavior. This word identified what the enemy was trying to do by causing me to fear man. God continued the work in me that He had started the year before while ministering to the women in the Dominican.

The word of God always goes to the giver first. My nature at times was to go along to get along, smile even when I wanted to say something else. I was never taught how to proclaim what belonged to me without feeling guilty for asking for what was mine. Here we are, talking about women having the right to do the work of the ministry without hesitation to preach and teach the gospel, lay hands on the sick, do the work of the ministry, just like a man?! No, just like a WOMAN! Not with the heart to compete with the man, for God made us complete in Him so we don't have to compete, but we are to walk alongside him in unity and harmony!

I did not know what the outcome or what would happen in the Conference in the Dominican Republic but God did. All He needed was a yielded vessel that would not look at her limitation but at God's impartation in her life. God has used me to minister this particular message across the country to women and men everywhere to set the captives free as He called me to do and with the same results, women of God are discovering their purpose, that they are indeed Women by Design!

Confession:

Father I thank you that you have given me power to walk through my process. I have Power, I'm on Purpose I am Designed!

A Little Color Can Bring Life to Any Surface; So Can a Little Make-UP! It's ok Ladies!

Designer Original

Oh yes, you shaped me first inside, then out!

In the beginning God! This book is dedicated to those women of God that have been standing still trying to figure out what their purpose is in life. Many women are trying to figure out; where I belong? Why am I here? When will I get there? These questions often asked by women have never been answered until now. Although I might have a six figure income or drive an expensive car or even live in a big house who am I and where do I belong? Why do I feel a gap in my development?

A well know prolific author named Dr. Miles Monroe, coined the phrase, "Without understanding the purpose of a thing, abuse is inevitable." I believe that he meant abuse is bound to happen when we don't understand and appreciate the value and reason for a thing or our purpose.

This powerful phrase lets us know without pause, if we want to understand our purpose as women, we must without fail acknowledge and diligently seek God who is our creator, our builder and our maker. The word of God says in Psalm 100:3, "...it is He that has made us, and not we ourselves." Therefore we must consult the maker of us to determine the purpose of us, the why for which we were made.

Genesis 1:26-28 says, "And God said, Let us make man in our image, after our likeness; and let them have dominion over the fish of the sea, and over the fowl of the air, and over the cattle and over all the earth, and over every creeping thing that creepeth upon the earth," Ladies we even have power over the creeps. "So God created man in his own image, in the image of God created he him; male and female created he them. And God blessed the man, (mankind) God said unto them be fruitful, and multiply, and replenish the earth. And subdue it; and have dominion over the fish of the sea and over the fowl of the air, and over every living thing that moveth upon the earth."

Now that we have the word of the Lord, let's take a closer look at what God says concerning His creation called woman and look at who the author of our life is. According to the Easton's Bible Dictionary, the name of the Divine Being in the rendering of the Hebrew EI_, from a work meaning to be strong; Eloah or Elohim. The Hebrew word Jehovah – a word used to denote the Supreme Being – is uniformly rendered as Lord. I particularly like the Barker Theology of the Bible definition, "THE Single Deity that Embodies the Entirety of Divine Life." To me that says it all! He is the Man, the Godhead!

God is the one that makes the rules, decisions and judgement for the purpose of life, His creation. He does not make us comply with His plan and purpose because life is choice driven. However, God has given us the power to choose just like He did Adam and Eve. He has set the rules and guidelines that govern our lives, the order, if you will, so that we can live our lives without chaos and we must be clear, the choice is ours to obey God or not. Let us get an understanding because no matter what else we get we need a clear perspective, an understanding! We must get an understanding of how and why we are who we are and that comes from Father God. James 1:5 says, "if any man lacks wisdom, let him ask God who will freely give it to us!" So now that we have that in view, let's look at the rest of what God has to say about His creation, woman.

It is the most wonderful thing in the world to know that God cares so much about us that He made us Designer Originals. Designer Originals are fashionable or luxury clothing made by or carrying a label of a well-known fashion designers. One of the main differences between designer clothing and other types of clothing is the quality of the materials and techniques and methods used to ensure high quality products will be produced and of course the designers name.

Certainly there are clothing brands that are not as pricy as what's called designers and of good quality also however the branding and the name associated with those clothes do not reach the level of notoriety and esteem as a designer item. Now a fashion designer is someone that not only makes clothes but also loves to study fashion trends, they select materials, sketch designs, and they have an overall part in all the production aspects of their design. They contribute to the creation of millions and I dare say billions of pieces of clothing and accessories according to Collins dictionary and sokanu.com. I wanted us to have a glimpse of what a Designer does because everything we see today is a reflection of what God has already done in the beginning.

Fashion designers look at trends or fads and decide what will be hot for the next season however God looks at Himself and says that all He has made is good and very good! We don't have to be a copycat of each other or be envious or jealous because our God the Original Creator and Designer made us all originals distinctly different, divinely designed and purposed to please Him. That's what makes us a designer original! Simply because we were designed, by an Authentic Originator!

Scripture tells us that Jesus is the Author and Finisher of our lives (faith) (Hebrews 12:2). There is a program on television that gives the viewer a close look at what it takes to become a model in a very competitive world of fashion. Now we know that models are the ones that have the distinct honor of wearing these designer clothing with the express purpose of showing off the clothing so that they can be seen, sold and satisfy the customer. The purchased and marketed outfit will then been talked about or publicized and repurchased over and over again

Again this process is similar to our walk as women of God. Let us look at many of the hardships that a model goes through to wear today's top fashions. The model, usually must be very thin and properly groomed and shown how to walk, talk and pose. They have to be taught people skills so they can become a complete marketing machine. Sometimes a model needs to diet or develop a systematic way of eating to get a desired result, usually weight loss to fit into the designer clothing. They have to give themselves completely to the project of getting fit in order to fit into the designer item and meet the goals set by the designer.

Models many times must adhere to tight, regimented deadlines to accomplish the ultimate results. The hard work many times pays off with them reaching their dreams of a modeling contract, fame and fortune. Women of God, we too have an assignment. The word of God says God would reward those that diligently seek Him, (Hebrews 11:6), we as women of God have to adhere to a strict diet of the word of God and put on the Lord Jesus Christ so that we can walk down the runway of life giving glory to God!

We are on a marketing campaign of letting our light shine so that men can see our good works and give glory to God!! Our deadline is when we meet God however, until then we are living epistles seen and read of men (women). When we allow God to groom us with His word it helps us get ready for the position and purpose He ordained for us in the earth. We will know the fulfillment of being who God says we are and doing what God says we can do and having what God says we can have. Like a top model, part of the preparation we need as women is the assurance and the confidence in the designer that they have given us the right outfit to wear on the runway of life. Have you ever seen a model not properly styled and her clothes not properly fitting? It makes for an awkward moment.

Therefore it is so very important that the relationship between the model and the designer are in agreement and in sync with each other having a congruent relationship. We must have the confidence to know that the outfit God gave us – a female earth suit is the right one! I like how the message version of the bible sums up Psalm 139:13-24, Oh yes, you shaped me first inside, then out; you formed me in my mother's womb. I thank you, High God- you're breathtaking! Body and soul, I am marvelously made! I worship in adoration-what a creation! You know me inside and out, you know every bone in my body; exactly how I was made, bit by bit, how I was sculpted from nothing into something. Like an open book, you watched me grow from conception to birth; all the stages of my life were spread out before you, the days of my life all prepared before I'd even lived one day. Selah (pause and clamly think of this).

"And ye are complete in him..." Colossians 2:10 Yes, we are complete in Him! God has made us complete in Him- nothing missing nothing broken. The key is in Him. Have you ever thought about why women love fashion so much? Why, do we spend so much time getting ready to go to the store or anywhere that we will be seen?! Why do we want and need hair, nails and nice clothing?! I believe it is because God made us that way!

Genesis 2:21-22 the Lord says, "And the Lord God caused a deep sleep to fall upon Adam, as he slept; He took one of his ribs, and closed up the flesh instead thereof; and the rib, which the Lord God had taken from man, made He a woman, and brought her unto the man." This scripture shows us this intimacy, (private time with God) you know ladies how we like that alone time with ourselves, mate etc., could this be the reason why because we were alone with God as we were being fashioned? This is the only time recorded in the word of God when man was asleep and only the woman and God were awake.

The woman spent time with God outside of the man, alone with God, without any interruptions or overrides available to hinder or suggest any revisions of God's perfect plans for her design. Can you imagine ladies, how it might have felt to be alone with the Creator, Father God, being designed? Well we were.

God put Adam to sleep, while He fashioned her, woman! We don't know how long he was sleep but the scripture says in Adam all were made alive. Adam includes the woman that represents all women that were to come. He didn't ask man's opinion, his thoughts or ideas at that time for the purpose of the woman, nor is God asking now! We don't have to be indifferent we just need to see that God already gave us identity, He made what he made! After, He fashioned her, and brought her to Adam, God, according to the Message version, presented her to him, then He asked Adam what do you say about my creation in other words to agree with Him and His purpose for the new being that was like Adam but was different and outside of him. God knows why

He fashioned you to be You!

The word made in Genesis 1:22 (in the original language) means to fashion or build, to build up, built again, According to Strong's concordance, this is the first mention of this word in scripture. It also identifies the word builder as the same understanding used when it comes to God Himself, who is our maker and builder according to Hebrews 11:10. In, Genesis 2:20 the word of the Lord says, "...but for Adam there was not found a help meet fit for him," The word, meet means to help assist, to aid, to build; fit suitable, pliable. No one else could meet the standard necessary to answer Adams' aloneness, so God made You, Woman!

You know ladies, we like our clothing to fit us. God wants us to understand that He knows what a good fit feels and looks like and we need to stop second guessing ourselves when it comes to fulfilling His call on our lives. We do fit in His plan for this earth, we are a part of God's original plan; His blueprint that determines the destiny of many. Proverbs 31:25-31 in the NLT says, "She is clothed with strength and dignity and she laughs without fear of the future. When she speaks, her words are wise and she gives instruction with kindness. She carefully watches everything in her household and suffers nothing from laziness. Her children stand and bless her. Her husband praises her; there are many virtuous and capable women in the world but you surpass them all! Charm is deceptive, and beauty does not last; but a woman who fears the Lord will be greatly praised. Reward her for all she has done. Let her deeds publicly declare her praise." You are that woman, own it! Strike a Pose!!!

Confession:

I am complete In Him, I have no lack, I have no fear. All that God made me to be I freely receive and possess!

I am built to last!

A Daily Dose of the Word of God, Worship, Prayer, Peace, Quite & Bubbles, Will Refresh the Spirit, Soul & Body!

Woman By Design ~ Woman On Purpose

Fashioned for Greatness!

"No one can measure His greatness…"

As I was walking on the treadmill this morning, the Lord began to tell me to tell you that you are fashioned for greatness! Greatness is not a simple objective, but greatness is the reflection of the training and order learned from your teacher, mentor, coach, parent, pastor or life. When I was a child, my mother always made sure I did certain household chores and that I learned some practical life lessons.

My mother Ruth was an amazing woman that could tell you all about yourself at first glance. We often thought that she was being mean but we have since come to realize that it was a gift of discernment and protection for our well-being from God to identify things that were from God and those things that were not! She was sharp and focused, an awesome singer, wonderful cook; and didn't stand for foolishness!

I remember when my mother taught me the importance of washing my hands (thank God) before I leave the bathroom as a young girl. I tried to reason in my young mind why I didn't think it was necessary. I even tried to let the water run so I could trick my mother into thinking that I had obeyed when I hadn't, but she being my teacher, and wanting the best for me was so much smarter than I was. She would wait outside the restroom and when I opened the door and told her I did what she told me to (which I hadn't). She would tell me to do it again, this time with the door open so she could see. What a wise woman she was. After a while, I began to think to myself, this is stupid, if I am going to turn the facet on, let the water run, I might as well stop being rebellious, put my hands under the water and wash them.

Wow when I think about the lesson that I needed to learn but also that she had to have the discipline and willingness to train and teach me. I was a child and I didn't know or understand but she was right there to prepare me for life. I know this life lesson might sound a little elementary for some but life itself is a classroom. It teaches us many things; how to live a dying defeated broken existence following the world's standards or how to live an intentional purpose driven victorious life following God's standards!

A little sidebar, I ended up working at the American

Medical Association in 1988 and while at the Association one of the departments that I worked in handled OSHA fulfillment requirement information. (OSHA) is THE Occupational Safety and Health Administration which was a Federal agency. Its responsibility was to monitor and enforce workplace health and safety regulations. One of the number one safety regulations in the work place was CLEAN hands! They required hand washing or hand hygiene on a regular basis to comply with their standards. So the lessons that my mother had already taught me caused me to be equipped and prepared and appreciate hand hygiene as an OSHA liaison.

Life is a classroom and circumstances can cause us to abort God's perfect plan simply by not submitting to His authority, orders and instructions. He says I desire obedience rather than our so called sacrifice. God gives us the answers to life's questions, although Adam and Eve missed it in the garden, we don't have to live a life of substandard living by following their example. We can choose to be obedient to God's directives. Jesus came! That's right J.E.S.U.S. came, that we might have and enjoy life and that more abundantly (John 10:10). Not just have life, but have and enjoy life More; a Godly life; a Great Life; an Abundant Life!

I was like many of you that thought I could not have the wonderful things that God's Word says I can have. I was actually told that by a preacher once. He said, I believe God for too much, and that I wanted too much from God! Can you believe that? That destroyed my momentum of my faith, my confidence and the value of my voice for a long time, so I thought. I literally stopped believing God! I stopped asking and I stopped dreaming because I was told by someone I trusted and respected, whom I thought knew better than I did how to approach God and ask for His will for my life.

I got the impression from this Pastor, that I shouldn't keep asking God for His best as it related to anything other than Jesus because it was as if I was annoying God, that might not have been what or how he meant what he was saying, however, that's how I received it. I felt that he was saying I could have Jesus but that should be enough. Looking back I went into a season of drought regarding my faith. The feeling that I was not important enough wouldn't leave me.

WOW! I experience a wound on my soul that would later be healed. I mentioned before, that I stopped dreaming about the things that I believed God could and wanted to do in my life as a young girl into being a young woman which I was at that time, and that wound continued into my adulthood.

Many women have been afflicted and never got healed yet, that's right I said yet. (We believe God for your healing right now to be released by the blood of Jesus, from whatever hurt that you have encountered in Jesus name)! I just didn't pray about the will of God for my life as a young Woman. Just general things you know like church and what to wear but not God's Purpose for me as a Woman!

Like many women today, we are so adaptable to life's big ideas, confirming to the world' system and ways of doing, flowing whichever way the wind blows that we don't conceptualize the idea that God might have a plan for our life. We might get a word from the Lord and act at the time on it not realizing that God's word is life and should continue to fuel us from faith to faith through His assignment for us in the earth. The word of life that He gives will not return void or empty of purpose but it will accomplish what He pleases and prosper in every way God sends it out too (Isaiah 55:11).

Although, I had gone through many unfulfilled years in my faith walk, God is always faithful! One day while the television was on a Christian station, I was going about my usual Sunday morning ritual of getting ready for church service when from another room I heard the preacher on the television preaching an incredible word! I was captivated by what I was hearing, backed into that room and didn't want to move. As I said, I was getting ready for my own church services and had to stop, sit down and listen. The word of God was feeding my soul and watering my spirit; my spirit man was charged up and I couldn't move away from the front of the television set until the program was over. That Pastor was Apostle, Dr. I.V. Hilliard. Oh my God! The scales began falling off my eyes and faith began springing up in my heart again, like receiving a cup of fresh water I was revived.

Faith began peeking through the clouds of doubt and fear. You might ask – fear; why fear. I had become accustom to not expecting God to move for me in a great way and I was afraid to believe again. I was afraid to dream again. The word of God that I was hearing from was breathing life into my spirit and causing me to believe again. He taught the word of God with such clarity and passion that it literally arrested my heart with a feeling of surrender and submission to God's word and will rose within me. The more I listened to the word of God the more I realized that I had been ripped off of my inheritance – my destiny for years.

Now let me make it clear I am and was then a Senior Pastor. But even in answering the call of God to Pastor alongside my husband Dr. Grant, the enemy's voice in my mind dispatched great words of discouragement often causing me to second guess the call of God on my life such as how can a husband

and wife or man and woman pastor together? I was walking in faith but I was questioning the faith that I was walking in. The enemy even would try replaying old sayings I'd heard like "anything that has two heads is a monster." God's word speaks to us of a Godhead which consists of three separate beings that functions in complete oneness. 1 John 5:7 says, "For there are three that bear record in heaven, the Father the Word and the Holy Ghost; and these three are ONE!" This doesn't sound like a monster to me.

The very day that I saw the television program, my wonderful husband and I were the overseers of an awesome church. I have loved the Lord all of my life. I have eight wonderful children (four by birth and four through the marriage of my children), and at the time nine grandchildren yet, I felt that I was not dressed for greatness. I was clothed with doubt, fear, and unbelief in who God made me. I didn't have faith working in my life in a great way, I had some faith but not great faith yet. I had a lot of hit and miss episodes, so I was not confident in who I was as a woman But when I heard the word of God from this clear, prophetic prolific powerful voice, it compelled and propelled me to put on the Lord Jesus Christ and make no more room (excuses) for the flesh (Romans 13:14). Belief began to Rise Up in me! Faith took over and again transformation happened.

You see, it is walking in line with God's word, believing we receive when we pray that will clothe us with greatness! Without faith we can't please Him. That's how we become fashioned for greatness, by putting on the word of God and letting faith come. We must become a doer of the word and not just a hearer (James 1:22). Not submitting to His order and plan for our lives, will simply leave us looking for a fig leaf to cover ourselves which is simply an excuse for disobeying God and man's poor substitute for a covering when God wants us to be clothed with His Glory!

Many of us – like I did with my mother will turn the water on in our lives we will go through the motions, some call it religion but won't put our hands under the water to wash them. We won't get fully engaged in the process of letting God have His way in us. We will read the word of God but won't do the word; we will do good things but are afraid to do great things! We will walk but won't run; we will talk but won't sing! It's time to allow the full measure of the power of God to flow through us, unhindered and unapologetic for being who He called you to be woman on purpose.

Greatness, according to the American Heritage College Dictionary, is defined as: remarkable or outstanding in magnitude, degree or extent; of outstanding significance or importance; superior in quality or character; powerful; influential. Thus, we see it will always give pause to something that is simply good. Don't get me wrong, good is good if that's your best, fair is also better than nothing, but a great job will always outshines a good job in life. The word of God says in Psalm 145:3 "Great is the Lord, and greatly to be praised; and his greatness is unsearchable. "Great is the Lord! He is most worthy of praise! No one can measure His greatness..." (NLT) As He is so are we, get ready to walk in your garment of greatness.

You and I my sister are made in His image and after His likeness. We too have the nature of greatness in our bones and in our DNA but we must be willing to leave the fashions of fear, despair, doubt, and unbelief and begin to walk in your true greatness. Believe the report God has releases concerning you. He gave us a documented pattern to follow.

Woman was presented to Adam as a crown of God's creation to bring him from a state of incompleteness or aloneness to a state of fulfillment. She was fashioned by God to be a partner so that what was in him could now walk beside him and they could rule together. She was the answer to Adam no longer being along. And God said it was not good for man to be alone, all one, so God made a helper that was just right for him. He knows you by name and God wants you to embrace that name and His plan for you!

God loves you with an everlasting love; you are so much better that good. That's right! You are better than just good, and the Lord God saw everything that He had made it was good, it was Very Good! My God! Girl you are good!

Confession:

Today I choose to walk in my Greatness, Value my Voice and Walk in my Worth. I am who God says that I am, I can do what God says I can do, I will have, what God says I can have because as He is so am I!

For A Woman, Life Brings About Many Challenges, but You Don't Fear Because When You're Thinking is Straight, You Know How to Change Hats!

Can't Take My Eyes off You!!!

With God all Things are Possible!

Have you ever seen a sister dresses so sharply that you scoped, peeped, looked at her from head to toe in one glance. Everything is in its place and you know that she knews that she looks good! My Mother Ruth was just such a woman. She loved being sharp and she didn't mind letting you know that she knew that she was sharp. That's also true for of Dr. Bridget Hilliard. She is always dressed sharp, which is one of the things that got my attention about her, not just what she wears outside, but her kind spirit also represents a well, dressed woman!

Just too good to be true; I can't take my eyes off you! These are some of the words of a song that describes a person not being able to look away from someone they found attractive. The word of

God says that God saw what He had made, that it was Good and very good! He not only saw the outside countenance or your earth suit, but He saw and still sees the heart. When we speak of the heart you know we are not just talking about the vessel in our bodies that pumps blood, but we are speaking of the inner core of mankind that governs our actions it is our believeth system. The believing part of us that causes confessions to be made into what we believe.

The bible in the Old Testament according to one source, speaks of the heart over 800 times and about 200 times its dealing with our emotions, or thought life, the very thing that motivates us to do what we do in life. The scripture says out of the abundance of the heart the mouth speaks, so our mouth responds to the wellspring of our heart. Our heart is often interchanged with the word mind or thoughts. It is again the core of our being what we think how we feel why we do what we do is all interwoven in our heart/thought/mind. "As a man thinketh in his heart, so is he" (Proverbs 23:7).

Our attitude is controlled by our thoughts, our emotions, how we feel, and how we function, are all the result of what is directing our thought life. How we perceive is how we believe something. (Romans 12:2)…be transformed by the renewing of our heart. It also says that we should guard, protect and cover your heart for out of it flows the issues of life (Proverbs 4:23), This scriptures gives us some insight on guiding our heart; Keep your mouth free of perversity; Keep corrupt talk far from your lips, Let your eyes look straight ahead, Fix your gaze directly before you.

The word says, "Give careful thought to the paths for your feet and be steadfast in all your ways. Do not turn to the right or the left; keep your foot from evil" (Proverbs 4:27). Everything we do in life comes as a result of what is in our heart. God says, "Man looks on the outward appearance, but God looks at the heart". In Matthew 22:37-39 (NLT) it says, "Jesus replied, You must love the Lord your God with all your heart all your soul and your entire mind. This is the first and greatest commandment. A second is equally important; Love your neighbor as yourself."

Now a command is an order given by one that has authority. It also means a signal that initiates an operation defined by an instruction. God has given us a command to love ourselves. Many times I find that we as women don't complete or fulfill our assignment is the earth because we refuse to see ourselves as God sees us. Woman have on so many levels been the best at being every woman; the cook, cleaner, driver, referee, babysitter on and on and on and the One thing in many regards that we have overlooked is taking care of ourselves! We have cared about and for everyone and everything else but have forgotten about One thing, Self-care the ability to care about ourselves, our goals, dreams, passions and purpose in the earth.

I've had the awesome privilege of working alongside my husband as I shared Dr. Grant Allison III for over 25 years now in ministry. Although God has used him in incredible ways to push me in the ministry and encourage me to go through doors I would not have gone through, I still struggled at times with some of doors I went through because of being a woman and the perception of others because I am a woman.

One of our members past away several years ago. The member requested that my husband and I do officiate at her home going services but her mother, who was not a member of our church wanted the services conducted at her church. We considered that church a more traditional church, which is the type I grew up in, than our church, (which, there is nothing wrong with traditional churches) however, the traditions being taught is what makes the difference. We didn't want to make an already difficult time of losing a love more difficult, we didn't want to argue with a grieving family even though they knew the loved one wanted her services at our location so we agreed to allow the services to be moved to their church location.

Sidebar, this is why it is so important ladies to have your wishes written down in some form a will or insurance policy some method so that your wishes would be honored in case something changes in life and what you want will be known and followed. The day of the services, we arrived early as we usually do for such services and someone came to get my husband to escort him to the pastor's office. I stayed in the sanctuary until he returned and he had a funny look on his face, not funny as in happy but like disappointed, displeased, and disturbed. I asked him what happened, he didn't want to say anything, but I knew they didn't want me in the pulpit area.

My husband told the pastor, "We conduct home going services together, so what are you saying?" The pastor responded to my husband, "I don't allow women in my pulpit." Again, my husband said, "So what exactly are you saying to me?" Now my husband knew exactly what the pastor meant, but it became somewhat of a standoff, you know when you can't believe what someone is saying or doing and you're giving them an opportunity to make a better decision? Can he really say he is a man of God and not be willing to obey God when being confronted? I knew from previous situations just like this one, to just stay out of the way and allow the Holy Spirit to work through my husband in order for God's will to be done. I didn't have to jump up and down and show anyone that I was capable as a woman to do the work that God had called me to do.

Finally, the pastor consented to allow me to sit in the pulpit and assist my husband officiating the service. This is one of the hardest times that I had to endure prejudice as a woman Pastor, I too was grieving the member that had passed away in addition to the behavior from the church pastor. I know what ever area of work we are involved in as women there are challenges associated with us being women however we are intentional, we are purposed and we are powerful! As I was seated in the pulpit and service was getting ready to start, I felt someone staring at me, I didn't know who or where it was coming from but I felt uncomfortable, you know that feeling you get when something is not quit right you're not sure what.

Now I had already gone through the storm of my husband dealing with the pastor so I thought it should be smooth sailing from here on out right, no wrong! I looked up after getting my notes together and I see this young man about fourteen years old looking at me with such malice, I could not believe it. No I wasn't preaching the service I was just sitting in the pulpit and assisting my husband. This young preacher was already being groomed to walk outside the will of God and had already formed an opinion about the role of a woman should be in the church. He thought that she had a place and it wasn't up there! He was being taught to ignore the bible that he had in his hand and follow the winds of doctrine that promoted sexism being taught seeing him behave like this; it was grievous to say the least. He didn't take his eyes off of me! The entire time I sat in the pulpit this young man glared at my every move, I mean he was watching, until I opened my mouth

He then began to look confused. How can this creature in a different earth suit that I am wearing have an anointing on her life like the men? How can God use her? I don't know if that's what he thought but his body language spoke volumes. Isaiah 10:27 says, "The anointing will destroy the yoke;" that includes male and female yokes. This young man was not the only one staring at me, the females in the choir also had the same look of displeasure as they saw me enter the pulpit, you know ladies how we can treat each other at times, I couldn't look at them either. I had no backup from the sistas! I had to do what God's word says, in Hebrews 12:2, "Looking unto Jesus, the author and finisher of my faith..." the amp says to "look away from all that will distract."

No matter what we are called to do in life we will have obstacles, and those obstacles can become our tomb stones or we can make them our stepping stones. God made them male and female to become all that He intended them to be therefore, we much stay focused on our assignment from God

Many of the members of my church (including the daughter of the member that passed away) apologized for the behavior of some of the people at that traditional church. They confirmed that the people in the church could not take their eyes off of me not for the good but because of not being taught God's word concerning Him using women to preach or do whatever He wants them to do.

I hear you women, saying, well I don't have a husband or a man to open doors for me Yes you do! You have the man Jesus Christ! He can open doors that no other man can close and close doors that no other man can open. On another occasion, one of my brothers did almost the same thing. God has used men I don't even know to open doors in the same manner.

The point is what God has called you to do in the earth as a woman might not always get good attention from man because they are looking at the outer appearance, but when you have God's attention you can still get the job done. What God calls you too, He will bring you through! Apostle I.V. Hilliard often says, "God is obligated to tell you the things you need to know and bring you into the company of the people you need to know that are critical for your success and destiny in life." I realized that this is the will of God for every woman to walk on purpose to fulfill the mandate that she has been given by God. You can accept the call, you must accept the call and you must walk in the will and the call of God. You have to make up your mind, no matter what; you will please God with the gift and talent that He gave. You must be willing to walk in the grace and with the guts to not be afraid or if you are afraid learn to do it afraid because you must do it anyway. Sometimes walking in the grace as a woman will bring fear but again do it anyway and watch God work through you and bless you to be a blessing!

God is searching the earth not just looking for a male man, but for those who's hearts are right toward Him. A corrupt heart according to Genesis 6:5 is the reason that God had to send the flood, so, we don't want that kind of flood but we want a flood from God that causes the will of God to manifest His blessing on and through us. That's always the plan of God for His daughters and the entire world to bless them. You have the necessary accessories to get the job done. God on.. strut your spiritual style; The world is watching but more importantly God has His eyes on YOU!!

Confession:

Lord I will trust you because you have made me in your likeness and your image and you will not allow anything to hurt or harm me, You are my God!

Real Beauty is the Result of a Clean Heart not Just A Sharp Outfit!

All Dressed Up!!!!

"He set the royal crown on her head, and made her Queen!"

Have you ever got all dressed up to go to an event and something happened that you were not able to attend? Did you feel unfulfilled, incomplete, cheated or plan empty? Well that is what happens when we walk in the anointing that God has given us as women and cannot participate in His purpose. We have learned how to get by; we put our spiritual outfit away in a nice clean garment bag and continue to say, one day I will wear my new outfit, one day, I am going to wear those sharp shoes. My sister today is the day to pull out your bad hat of salvation; that outfit of worship, your sharp shoes of the gospel and your garment of praise that breaks yokes of heaviness and go to the event called life where God can use you for

His glory.

of us are called into the pulpit, or like Queen Esther to the palace. Remember she was an orphan; she had lost her mother and father and was living with her uncle who had raised her. She was beautiful and when the king sent out a decree for a new wife Esther the orphan was swept up in the group of young women being considered, the scripture doesn't even tell us that she wanted a husband and especially not the king.

Like all the other young women in that season, Esther was being looked at and she got favor with a person name Hegai, who was the one in charge of the women. Because she pleased him, she received kindness from him and he gave her the things that she needed to get prepared for the purification process and then possibly come before the king. Wow!

We all have to go through a purification process in our lives to allow the Holy Spirit to address any areas in that are not pleasing to God so that we can get rid of them and we too will come before the King of Kings. One of the first things they did was to discard the old cloths, which for women is wounds like old mindsets, thoughts of inferior, inadequacy and insecurities, rejection, bitterness, loneliness and the list goes on. The process Esther went through was 12 months long but for some it might take 12 years, or 24 years or like Sarah 25 years before her promise seed was born. Anna was an intercessor that served in the temple praying night and day for the coming of the Lord, she had been married for several years and then her husband died and the rest of her life she spent in the temple as an intercessor. That was her assignment and she fulfilled it.

We don't always know how or when or why, but when we know God we don't have too we can trust Him that in the right season and the right time or the fullness of time, we will know what we need to know that is critical for our success and destiny in life! Esther received favor above all the other candidates in the eyes of the king and he set the royal crown on her head, and made her Queen. Her very crown was an indication of her authority and power in the kingdom, so it is as women of God, our crown of righteousness also identifies that we are our heavenly father's daughter.

A quote so often used from the book of Esther is when her uncle was trying to encourage her to not be afraid to go before the king to help her people that were on the verge of being destroyed and he said, "For if thou altogether holdest thy peace at this time, then will relief and deliverance arise to the Jews from another place, but thou and they father's house will perish; **and who knoweth whether thou art not come to the kingdom for such a time as this?"** (Esther 4:14).

Oh my God this scripture is everything! It speaks to the very heart of women everywhere! Some that are in the market place and some in corporate America or in the Hospital rooms, teachers, doctors, nurses, housewife, truck drivers, beauticians, and of course mothers, where ever God has called you to serve in the earth He has equipped you for the assignment for which you have been called to for such a time as this!

Do you remember, when everyone used to get their clothes ready on Saturday for Sunday morning service. Well at least at my mother's house we did. We could not wait until Sunday morning to get our clothes ready, or our hair done, we had to have everything in order on Saturday night. Our baths included, everything had to be ready so that we would be left without an excuse Sunday morning. Mother didn't want us to miss our appointment with God which she felt was the most important thing we would do all week long.

In my house my mother was in charged. She was a divorced single mother of ten children. I have six brothers (5 of which are older than me) and three sisters (all are older than me). I could tell them all day to get ready for church and they wouldn't move, I was not the boss of them, but if I said mama said, that made all the difference in the world. It didn't matter if you had a stomach ache or you didn't like the outfit that you had to wear, once mama said it, you were going to church. I hear the same clarion call for this hour for the women of God! Only this time it's not just mama saying it, but it is God Almighty saying to His daughters, I have called you for such a time as this to show forth my glory in the earth.

Don't look to the right or the left, but keep your eyes on me; keep your heart full of my plan for you so that you can overcome the fear of man. Don't look to the right or the left but straight ahead, look away from all that will destract. I am with you; I am here for you to bring you to an expectant end. Walk boldly before me and I will bring you into your wealthy place. I am not a man I will not lie. I have commanded and I will stand by my Word!!!

I have four children; my oldest is a wonderful woman of God and three incredible men of God. There are times when I go to the mall or the grocery store and one of their friends that I have never even met would ask me if I know one of my children. I always respond yes, I know them, but how did you know they are my children. They always would respond without fail and say, "Because you look just them." Of course we know they look like me, seeing I am the parent but the point is, people, that I've never met were able to see the resemblance between me and my children although I did not know them. They spotted the alikeness that I had with my children because they looked like me.

We as women of God should have the same testimony; sons and daughters are supposed to look like our Father in all that we do, including ministry. For many years women have been mishandled, misunderstood, misused and considered second rate blabber mouths. We have been accused by some of our counterparts of trying to act like a man, trying to walk in a man's shoes, doing a man's job or just trying to be a man.

I remember preaching one day and after the service the pastor came and asked my husband, "How can you handle your wife knowing the word like that?" We couldn't believe our ears. As quite as it's keep, although it's in the word Jesus would often use women to assist Him in ministry. Luke 8:1-3 says, "And it came to pass afterward, that he went throughout every city and village, preaching and shewing the glad tidings of the kingdom of God: and the twelve were with him, And certain women, which had been healed of evil spirits and infirmities, Mary called Magdalene, out of whom went seven devils, and Joanna the wife of Chuza Herod's steward, and Susanna, and many others which ministered unto him of their substance."

That's right the women were with Jesus and they also supporting the work of Jesus out of their substance (money). WOW!

God our father gave us clear instructions as women just as he did the man, to be fruitful and replenish the earth. He fashioned us for greatness, He brought us to the man and in my own words said, this is your helper. She is suitable, adaptable, a builder, restorer, and nurturer. She is wise, bold, strong, kind, sharp, and courageous. She is tenderhearted, a healer, a mother, daughter, sister, granddaughter and a sister- friend. She is my daughter. She can stand by your side and help you but she can also stand alone! She knows how to subdue, multiply and replenish the earth. I created her to be just like me, in my image, after my likeness. I made her a builder, and every wise woman builds her house (Proverbs 14:1)!

A builder is one that constructs something by putting parts or material together over a period of time, a person whose job is to repair or contract for the construction and repair, on that creates or develops a particular thing according to the dictionary. She is my builder the Lord says! Part of building her house, includes not just washing the dishes and moping the floor, but it includes, walking in the anointing that I gave her as well.

I have learned many lessons from in my life one is that God has ordained us to follow those, who through faith and patience inherit the promise. Don't be sluggish but be bold and imitate them." I didn't even realize for some time that this is a scripture in Hebrews 6:12. I'm sure I had read it but it came alive when I saw a living example of how to walk this scripture out by faith. God has given us exceeding great and precious promises and as we embrace His will for our lives, we will discover that, "the blessing of the Lord makes us rich (abundantly supplied in every area) and he adds no sorrow to it" (Proverbs 10:22) (paraphrased) His anointing on you can set the captives free.

God wants you to know woman, that you are not an afterthought; you are part of His original plan and purpose. When I was a child we used to play a game called tag. During the process of playing the game, the objective was to tag the players and get as many people as possible out before the time ran out. We usually started playing the game around dusk, because when it got dark we couldn't see and it was difficult to continue playing. Well, God has an objective for women along the same lines. We must get in the Game. God wants as many of us as possible to get actively involved in working the works of Him that sent us while it is day because the night is coming and no man will be able to work (John 9:4).

Our mission on earth to walk as powerful women, will not be accomplished unless we move from complacency to action! The ability to judge what is right and then act on it some would say is wisdom... for wisdom has built her house...

(Proverbs 9:1) The reverential fear of the Lord is the beginning of that wisdom and the knowledge of the Holy one is understanding (Proverbs 9:10.

SO, I say to you woman of God, TAG YOUR IT! You are God's Chosen! Rise and Shine! You are purposed to please the King! You are a woman created by God! You are a Woman by Design, A Woman on Purpose!

Confession:

Father I receive your wisdom, I receive you strength and I receive your heart to walk out my purpose in the earth in Jesus name!

Next Steps:

If you have not accepted Jesus Christ as your Lord and savior, wow you are in the right place for an amazing transformative life to begin for you. God changes us from the inside out, a little at a time.

Jesus came and said, "God's Spirit is on me; He's chosen me to preach the Message of good news to the poor, He has Sent me to announce pardon to prisoners; and recovery of sight to the blind, to set the burdened and battered free, to announce, This is God's year to act!" (Message version). If by any chance, you are in any one of these categories, then it's your time to be made new to be set free. Gods says, if we can believe in our heart and make a real confession with our mouths that Jesus is the son of God then we can be saved Because with our heart we believe and with our mouth confession is made into salvation (Romans 10:9-10)!

What does this mean? It means that you are loved

by the father and He wants you to be part of the family. So just Repeat after me: Father I believe without Jesus I am lost, I need a savior and I believe Jesus is the son of God that came to save me from my sins, I want Jesus to be my savior I receive him Now and I thank you for making me whole in Jesus name I pray.

Now, confess with me that I am saved, I am free and I am a woman (man) of God!

I am a lover of God and a lover of His word and I read it every day and have always made confessions as I go. I pray you will also fall in Love with Him!

I came across A wonderful book by Dr. Bridget Hilliard called Wisdom for an Incredible Life which included these 15 freedom truths that I believe are designed to help establish and set your heart (fixed) upon the Word of God. I believe these truths will help you grow intentionally and spiritually! We walk by Faith (2 Cor. 5:7) and that Faith comes from hearing the word of God (Romans 10:7) therefore with permission from Dr. Bridget I included these confessions truths here.

I want you to be encouraged daily and read all of them or just use one a day if you like as your life is being transformed:

1. *I am a new creature, predestined for greatness (2 Cor. 5:17)*

2. *I am a child of God, fully accepted by the Father (John 1:12)*

3. *I am loved by God regardless of how I perform (Rom. 5:8)*

4. *I am forgiven and will not be tormented by my past errors (1 John 5:4)*

5. *I am an overcomer and my faith is changing my circumstances (1 John 5:4)*

6. *I am a giver and God is causing people to help me prosper (2 Cor. 9:8)*

7. *I have authority over the devil and no demon power can hurt me (Luke 10:17).*

8. *Abundance is God's will for me and I will not settle for anything less (John 10:10).*

9. *I am healed and sickness will not lord over my body (1 Peter 2:24).*

10. *God is on my side; I chose not to fear (Ps. 118:6)*

11. *The Holy Spirit is my helper and I'm never alone. I have the peace of God (Phil 4:7).*

12. I am blessed and it's only a matter of time before things change. What I see now is only temporary (Eph. 1:3; 2 Cor. 4:18).

13. I have the wisdom of God; I hear the Father's voice; my steps are ordered by God (1 Cor. 2:7; John 14:24; Ps. 37:223).

14. I am set in the Body of Christ and I know that I am valuable and important to the work of God (1 Cor. 12:20-25; Eph. 4:11).

15. I choose not to be offended and I am being delivered out of all afflictions and persecutions (Matt. 5:10-13).

My Prayer for You!

My Prayer for you woman of God is that your life will never be the same! Just like the women in the Dominican Republic, I pray and believe that your Purpose will spring forth like living water and quench your thirsty soul. I know that part of what God has called me to do in the earth is to Motivate, Inspire and Develop (MITW) Women to fulfill their God given Purpose and Destiny in Life. We Decree and Declare that you are a Woman by Design, A Woman on Purpose! We Decree and Declare, that you are blessed and highly favored! We break every chain of the enemy off your life now and we come out of agreement with his hold over your mind in Jesus name! I honor you and I am honored to serve the King with , we have been called to the Kingdom of God for such a time as this!

Abiding, In His Love, Dr. Renee

My Personal Life Confession!

www.ingramcontent.com/pod-product-compliance
Lightning Source LLC
Chambersburg PA
CBHW071159090426
42736CB00012B/2391